WORDS FOR THE JOURNEY

DAVID LUCAS & REBECCA PARNABY-ROOKE

TABLE OF CONTENTS

TABLE OF ILLUSTRATIONS

DEDICATION

Dave says:

This book would not have been possible without the inspiration of my two wonderful guide dogs, Abbot and Jarvis.

Together my boys have led me through the darkest of times, all the while teaching me the most valuable of lessons; to keep moving forward even when the road ahead is dark and full of unseen dangers. For such is the nature of faith. Even when God seems far away, we must place all our hope and trust in him, just as I did every time I left home in the care of one of these wonderful dogs.

Above all the boys have taught me that true faith is to put all your trust in the one who loves you, and to hurl yourself into the unknown darkness, not in any half-hearted or ultra-cautious way, but with all the enthusiasm you can muster, trusting that he will guide you, keep you safe and at the end of the day lead you safely home rejoicing.

If I had but one prayer for all of you, dear readers, it would be that you put all your trust in the One who loves you and allow him to bring you safely home. At any one time you may not know where it is he is leading you; you don't need to, nor does it matter. All that matters is that you give him your trust and enjoy the journey.

I owe my boys so much. Bless you, boys.

Rebecca says:
My involvement in this book is down to the inspiration I found in my beautiful husband James, who opened such doors for me to a whole new world of liberal theologies, and my fierce desire to create a better church for my children to experience. My family is everything and this is for you.

I also want to thank all the wonderful people I have journeyed with in the online space. I have learned so much from such a diverse group of amazing siblings. Inclusion blesses us all, and I have been truly blessed. Thank you.

PREFACE

We rarely pause to consider where words have come from: their history, root-meaning and what might lie behind them. So here, in the Preface – which I am humbled and honoured to be invited to write – let me unpack the two words that give us the title of this organisation: Ordinary and Office.

Our word 'ordinary' comes from the Latin and the Old French *ordinarie*, meaning regulated, customary, usual, arranged or regular. Five hundred years ago it had slipped a little in definition to indicate something or someone that was commonplace, common in occurrence, or not distinguished in any way. It also came to signify the lowest base; O-levels were 'ordinary' – there was nothing below them.

What then of our word 'office'? It too traces its meaning from the Latin, the word *officium* meaning a service, kindness and favour. It also meant some kind of obligatory service, or an official duty, function or business. The Latin root itself was connected to *opificium*, literally meaning 'work-doing', and was linked to power, might, abundance and means.

Jesus was born in an ordinary small town, to an ordinary couple, in an ordinary and unremarkable part of the Roman Empire. Later in life, Jesus will seek out more ordinary, common people. Jesus will tell parables about ordinary things. Jesus' kingdom is filled with ordinary people. Jesus heals the common people, not the privileged.

Jesus had an office. Not the modern kind, where you might work from nine-to-five. Jesus' office was his service, compassion, care, tenderness and goodness. Jesus, as the person God chose to be, was obliged to serve, welcome, love beyond measure, and to never cease in giving. His life was, and is, an expression of God's abundance, means and power. That power is love. It is gracious and freely given, and utterly inexhaustible.

One example of Jesus being, doing and embodying 'Ordinary Office' comes in

Chapter 13 of the Gospel of John, where Jesus does the ordinary, banal business of washing the feet of his disciples. This was the obligatory task of servants and slaves, and utterly unremarkable. The story John recounts concludes with Jesus saying, "You must love one another just as I have loved you." (John 13:34, NIRV).

It is arguably the greatest commission we have from Jesus; we are told we are his friends and we are called to follow his example. Granted, other words from Jesus might just as easily make a claim to be the Great Commission. What about "Love your neighbour as yourself" (Mark 12:31, NIV)? Or "Turn your other cheek" (Matthew 5:39, NIRV)? Or "Whatever you did for one of the least of these brothers and sisters of mine, you did for me"

(Matthew 25:40)?? What is your Great Commission? What is it that sends **you** out into the world with hope, joy, and a passion and calling to transform it?

The Christian faith contains a number of competitive theories as to what our main priorities should be. But there is a common thread that runs through them all, and it is this. Out of the ashes of Good Friday, of failure, defeat and tragedy, hope and new life are born. The disciples are called to be the ambassadors of the endless love, new hope and transformation that is wrought in the person of Jesus. Their example leads us to developing our own vocations through prayer and care.

The resurrection, in other words, was something that did not draw disciples so much into a new sect as it did send them out into the world, with joy, conviction, and a desire to serve the world and the needs of others in the name of the living Christ. Critically, this was done in love. This is not a task; it is an entire reconfiguration of our lives. You see, you cannot really command people to love. That's the catch. Love is for falling into and then living out of. It is a state of being, as well as doing.

Many of us who work in caring professions – perhaps especially in the church – are faced, daily, with a simple dilemma. How do we begin to complete and apply the task that our forebears bequeathed us? How do we bring resurrection and transformation to the base materials, situations and people that we are here to serve? How do we heal the sick, comfort the lost, illuminate the confused? How to bring hope, joy, peace and wisdom to those who are searching for, or needing, health, completeness or love?

Invariably, the things that inspire us – and here I choose my words carefully – are not the formal rules, regulations and codes that often govern our professions and institutions. I, for example, do not get especially excited by reading canon law, the Ordinal, or the bishop's latest ad clerum. What motivates and inspires me in my life is the example of others. What is set out and lived in the life of others is what can transform us and make us into better people ourselves. One Saint, in his own charge to his community, says, "Go and preach the Gospel throughout all the world…if absolutely necessary, use words…".

In the Christian faith, true religion is judged not by its seeds, but by its fruits. Christianity is known by what is reaped, not what is sown; love, holiness and discipleship are found in the bounty of harvest. Faith is not judged by its origins, but by its ends. Thus, Christians only have one thing to invest: their lives. The only possession we have – ourselves – is asked to be surrendered. We cannot truly give until we give up ourselves, and we cannot love unless we first know that we have always been loved.

Surely this gospel is too demanding? Brother Roger of Taizé used to reply to just that question with these words: "Il ne demande pas trop – mais il demande tout." ("He doesn't ask too much – but he does ask for everything."). Or as Jesus put it, "Love one another – as I have loved you." Our calling is no more and no less than following him and becoming like him.

So here is my charge as you read this book, and pray through it on your own, or with friends and fellow Christians. Become a living text. Be the Verb of God Made Flesh – let the spoken words of Jesus be fully expressed in your life, work and being. Become The Ordinary Office of God that Jesus was and is. To live your life like this is to do nothing more than ensure that others who spend time with you spend every day with Jesus too.

As you pray through these pages, let the grace and goodness of God surround you and fill you. Seek the lost. Pursue God's wisdom. Live a holy life. Offer your kindness and care to friends and strangers. Pray ceaselessly. Love all people strongly and tenderly, as God does.

Go in peace to love and serve the Lord. Be The Ordinary Office of Jesus wherever you are. God will bless you and bless others. For we are called to be The Ordinary Office of God.

The Very Revd. Professor Martyn Percy
Dean of Christ Church, Oxford

Lent 2022

I hear footsteps in the garden and I
know my Lord is near

WELCOME

To those who feel estranged from God we say, you are welcome.

To those who feel estranged from his church we say, you are welcome too.

To those who feel unwelcome we say, you really are very welcome.

To those who do not feel valued by church we say, no matter how the church has made you feel, you are welcome here. Your experience, your hurt, your pain and your opinions matter here.

To those who feel ignored we say, we recognise you and you are more than welcome here.

The Ordinary Office is the place for the dispersed, disenfranchised, dispossessed and estranged.

Be in no doubt that you are welcome here. We will go to great lengths and do our best to remove barriers in the way of your access to the prayer life of our community, so you can take part as much or as little as you choose. If we are failing in some way, we want to know about it, and to learn whether it be in our power to do something about it.

We are not so much inviting you to read a book or to say a set of prayers, but rather to share a journey. We invite you to travel with us for as long as you wish, be it just for today, or for a long time to come. Once again, we say you are welcome.

Stay for as long or as little as you like and together let us share the journey. Tag along in silence or chat away; the choice is yours. If you need an arm to link, it is here. If you metaphorically wish to sneak in quietly at the back and to be left unbothered until you feel comfortable introducing yourself, that is fine too.

We believe firmly in what sociologist of religion Peter Berger called 'the heretical imperative.' (Berger, 1979). No subject is off limits, there are no opinions or ideas that are not allowed. All we ask is respect and compassion for others in sharing.

If you have been damaged by bad teaching or theology, do not fear. Here we only have thoughts to offer, not dogma. What we are offering is the benefit of the things we have lived through and experienced on our own journeys. There is much we have learned but we offer it only for your consideration. Feel free to pull it apart, to scrutinise it, to see if it is a fit for you. Shake the box that is The Ordinary Office, see what falls out, embrace what works for you and disregard the rest.

This is no hard sell. Think of it as a catalogue full of many things. Some you may wish to own, some you might like simply to borrow for a while, some you may totally disregard and some you may come back to later.

Like a catalogue, you may wish to keep this book on a shelf and simply dip into it from time to time when searching for something new or to refresh a memory. It may just be enough to know that it is there on the shelf waiting for such a time as you may need it.

Dave says:
As a blind man who can no longer read physical books, I still own many treasured books that I keep on my shelves, no longer for what I can read within them, but for what they have meant to me, for what they represent.

Our prayer is that this book may be a blessing to you, not something else to burden you. God knows there is enough of that baggage out there already; Rebecca and I have both suffered enough through trying to adopt teachings and philosophies that were part of the canon we are all told we should study in order to fit in, yet knowing it wasn't in line with the Jesus we knew. We anticipate many of you will have shared this experience too.

So many Christian books have become almost compulsory reading. You know the ones everyone says you must have in order to belong, the ones you have to say were really deep and profound just to be part of the crowd. This is not one of those.

Keep it because it speaks to you in some way. If it doesn't, simply give it away and forget about it. In doing so you may bless another, and we trust God knows what he's doing!

Enjoy the journey, travel with us for as far (or as short) a distance as you like and, by the way, did we mention that you are very welcome?

It is the role of The Ordinary Office to bridge the gap between a traditional church which is all too often inaccessible to those disenfranchised by it, and the wider church of God's children seeking his promised love. It is our role to play our part and to make sure these communities are not forgotten.

INTRODUCTION

Dave again.

I am a child of the sixties, a baby boomer. I have grown up with what I like to think is a highly developed sense of cool - even if to look at me you may not think so.

For my generation image has been king. We have grown up with album covers, magazines, billboards, top brands such as Gucci shoes, Armani suits, Porsche cars. These are the things we have been conditioned to aspire to. You might say that all this is mere frippery and to a large extent you would be right. Nonetheless, the fact remains that image is important to all of us to some degree.

We all like, and indeed it could be argued, need to achieve a certain cool quota. Think of the crucifixion and the soldiers who drew lots for Jesus clothes because they were so fine and well made. Jesus valued cool too.

Why am I telling you this here? Well, take a look at things specifically designed for disabled people. Disabled people are being served up a whole array of products which are simply designed for function with little or no regard for form. Bright yellow keyboards with big letters for visually impaired people, chunky mobile phones, ugly prosthetics in only one (white) skin tone and so on. Look at the back of any Innovations Catalogue and you will see in full glorious colour a whole range of the kind of tasteless crap that I'm talking about.

All of this can eat away at the self-esteem of a disabled person. The prevailing attitude of designers seems to simply be that 'it does the job and they're disabled so what does it matter?' Well let me tell you as far as this disabled bloke is concerned it matters a great deal indeed. I would rather manage without something than be seen with some of the rubbish that is regularly offered to disabled people as a so-called solution.

When I thought about writing a Daily Office these were the thoughts that crowded my mind. There are very few books written with a pan-disability audience in mind, such that are written not just in simple language, which is good, but in juvenile language with no sense of the poetic. It is often as if the author thinks that disabled people have had a type of cultural bypass. Such books are usually printed with garish covers resembling something from the Early Learning Centre.

It has been my ambition to produce an office book that, although written in less complex and therefore more accessible language, still retained enough of the poetic to appeal to the inner poet in all of us. Then it was equally important that the book look attractive, something that I would not be embarrassed to be seen out with. It is my fervent hope that this book goes some way to meet those criteria. This book is a set of prayers that have grown out of my journey. Prayers of hope, prayers of lament, prayers of comfort, prayers that celebrate what it means to be an exiled person made in the image of God. This means yes, even sometimes prayers of anger and frustration, prayers that pull no punches in telling our God exactly how we feel. He is a big and mighty God, he can take it, in fact I believe he demands it. What he desires from us most is honesty.

These prayers have been influenced by those who I have met along the way, whose stories have become intertwined with mine and whose friendship I count as precious. Over time some of these prayers have grown into liturgies, which are now being said all over the globe more than six-thousand times a day by our online community at www.anordinaryoffice.co.uk.

As the journey continued, Rebecca joined me and brought a new dimension to the work of The Ordinary Office. This book is a way marker in our journey, so that others may follow as they make their own path.

A CRY FROM THE HEART

I posted a version of this prayer on Twitter (all be it in a somewhat simpler form) as a kind of open letter to the church from disabled people, and it has been retweeted literally hundreds of times.

We are scared Lord. The disenfranchised, those deemed unacceptable to the wider church, on grounds of ability, sexuality, gender or race. Those who force the church to have to look at herself. Those who we have allowed to be abused within it and who we are now too ashamed to look at.

We have been pilloried in the press, portrayed as benefit cheats, lawless, anti-establishment, scroungers and degenerate.

Many of us have spent more than two years shielding and locked down.

We listen to others say, 'Shield them and lock them down so that we can get on with our lives!' and we are supposed to see that as an act of care, an act of love! That is not how it feels.

During the pandemic we opened our hearts and welcomed the wider church community into our world, the world of online church. The world which we had already pioneered. The world that they had previously dismissed as invalid, not a true form of worship.

Now as the world rushes to go back to what is once was, we feel abandoned, forgotten, left behind. Our visitors rush back into their buildings and once again dismiss online church as not good enough, as lesser.

For generations we have looked to your church but we can't get in. We wait outside but we can't climb the stairs.

We peer through the stained glass from the outside wishing we felt part of the celebration taking place within.

The language and liturgies are too complex for many of us to understand.

The literature is not available in formats we can read.

The sound system is broken, there is no BSL signage. We cannot last the length of the service without need for a changing places loo, yet there are none.

There is no understanding of the theology of disability.

There are attitudes of prejudice both conscious and unconscious.

Our responses to the traumas triggered in our very souls from ill handled bible passages or interpretations of texts are misread as us 'being difficult'.

Our pleas for understanding, learning and change are seen as disruptive, and we are dismissed.

There is a lack of understanding of the spirit of mutuality.

We do not want to be there to have things done to us or for us but with us.

Bad, even toxic theology continues to hold sway.

We are told we are disabled because of our sin.

We are told we have not been praying hard enough or we would have been cured.

They push us in our wheelchairs into dark corners so that we are not 'in the way.'

We are asked to move because our service dog is leaving hair on the carpet.

Hands are laid on us in prayer without being asked for our consent.

We see far too few people like us at the front, leading the worship.

We welcomed you into our home online and you were glad of it for a while but are we now to be abandoned all over again?

We hear so much talk of safeguarding but who is watching out for us?

We are talked about in loud whispers as we enter the building that has been so hard to get in to in the first place.

People complain that disabled children are making too much noise during the service; families with disabled children are asked not to come back.

People complain that more accessible forms of worship are not traditional.

Children with learning disabilities are refused the sacraments because they 'may not understand' - but Lord, which of us fully understands the mystery of Your love?

We gather online not just because it is the most accessible way for us to be but also because we find this space much safer.

We are told that this is no substitute for 'real church'; this, Lord, from the church that cannot meet our needs yet reserves the right to criticise what we do for ourselves out on the margins.

Lord, we need to be heard by your church.

We need to feel love from your church.

Lord, we need your church to value us, to see that we have gifts to offer them, that we want to be there not just to be ministered to but to minister.

We have been hanging on for so long, Lord, yet after so many years we are still being told it will take such a long time. We hear that it is prohibitively expensive, that the historic architecture is too precious to make accessible and needs to be retained in its original state.

Are we not more precious than your buildings, Lord?

We look to the front but see no one like us at the altar.

We want to believe we are made in your image, Lord, but we look at your church and cannot see a reflection that looks like us.

Lord, where is hope?
Lord where is kindness?
Lord where is love?

When will we feel truly valued?

We don't know how much longer we can hang on, Lord.

We are tired.
We are weary.
We are dispirited.

We cry out, how long, Lord! How long!

Come to us now, Lord, and lighten this
darkness of ours.

Begin a new creation within your church,
Lord, show us that truly ALL are welcome.

Let it not just be the slogan at the bottom
of the church notice board but a
statement of TRUTH, a declaration of
Your LOVE!

This book is our letter to your church
Lord. A cry of the heart, a lament, a
modern-day psalm.

We offer you this very book, Lord, as our
prayer, a heartfelt plea for your tender
mercies.

Let them flow over us Lord, wash away
the status quo, and bring change. Amen.

WHY?

Dave here.
Welcome everyone.

The work I have done, formerly with Disability and Jesus on Twitter, and now with The Ordinary Office, has brought me into daily contact with not just disabled people, but many other groups who feel exiled from on-site church. People with mental health concerns, abuse and trauma survivors, LGBTQIA+ people, people of colour. People who are quite simply at the end of their rope with religious establishments. I need my church, the church I love, the church that gave me a home, the church to whom I owe so much, to understand.

This is not an attack on the church but a plea. A plea to come to the aid of those who have been exiled for so long their hope is beginning to fail. If we let them down, it will be an indictment on all of us.

At times, my words may seem harsh but please give me the benefit of the doubt. Justin Welby once referred to me as his critical friend and I earnestly pray that you are able to see that.

Every day my inbox is full. I get bombarded with letters, emails, Skype, Zoom and phone calls from these exiled people, the spiritually disenfranchised who are in search of hope, in search of a spiritual home.

You only just have to scratch the surface to discover a whole world of spiritual nomads, people made homeless by the church's lack of understanding and concern.

The work I have done on Twitter and through The Ordinary Office has simply been my feeble attempt to address this issue. I have no funding or resources; it has been just me. More recently joined by Rebecca, we serve with our time and our prayers. With just such poor resources we have built up a Twitter following of almost twenty-thousand, and more than six-thousand people regularly say The Ordinary Office prayers which have now been said more than 2.5 million times in just three years.

Imagine what could be done with the full weight of the wider church behind this work. Think what could be achieved by a well-resourced team who were not reliant on the church for their livelihood and home, therefore totally at ease to speak truth to power.

Imagine the tearing of curtains that could be done, the walls we could break down in the name of Jesus.

THIS BOOK

This book is largely meant as a keepsake. Although not set out in date format, it is meant as a kind of prayer journal.

If at the end of a year it is not looking slightly battered, the notes pages are not full of your scribblings and little keepsakes are not kept pressed within its pages then we encourage you to dive into it further in the next year.

Over time we will produce more new prayers and liturgies which you will be able to access – we don't intend to stop here. There is much work to be done, and we invite you along for the journey.

The aim is that this book will become a much-loved friend rather like your childhood Teddy; a bit threadbare and battered with all its fur rubbed off, but much loved.

The prayers gathered here are not meant to be a substitute for your own. We like to think of them as hopefully a way of 'priming the pump'. When prayer doesn't come, as it often doesn't for us, we hope that you can take these words and once again your own prayer will begin to flow.

There is a value in repetition. When we repeat certain phrases and even actions, like fingering prayer beads, we create a quiet rhythm within our spirits. The beating of our heart is a repetition as is the rhythm of our breathing. All of life has its rhythms and the repetition of familiar prayers can bring our interior spirits in to harmony with the Divine heartbeat and the breathing of the Divine Christ.

Stephen J Binz

WHAT IS THE ORDINARY OFFICE?

The Ordinary Office is a set of simple, accessible daily prayers based online where we know many of those exiled from organised church have begun to gather.

Over time those using The Ordinary Office have bonded into a sense of community, mainly on Twitter.

There are several liturgies on the site, all of which are available in print, in Widgit symbol form, in audio and on video. They are shared daily via links on Twitter. We also now share a weekly service on YouTube and Facebook.

COMMUNITY

This community is a rag tag and bobtail group of the lost, broken, estranged and isolated who interact with each other via Twitter chat, the occasional quiz or social event and the sharing of the prayers that make up our Daily Office.

There is no formal membership, it is open for anyone to join in and you can be as involved as much or as little as you wish to be.

We look forward to you joining with us each day as we pray the office and gather on Twitter, on our website and on YouTube or Facebook.

WHY AN OFFICE?

For almost forty years I (Dave) have been saying a Daily Office of one sort or another, from my old Catholic breviary which I began at 19 in my days in the seminary, through to the Northumbrian Office, now known as Celtic Daily Prayer, when it was in its infancy in the 1980s.

Often in times when God has seemed far away, or even sometimes not there at all, it has been saying the regular prayers of a Daily Office that has kept me in a strange way connected to God, even though in other ways it felt like I was not hearing from him at all. At times saying a Daily Office has felt like an act of glorious defiance, that somehow no matter what life has thrown at me, no matter how distant God may have seemed, I have shouted out my office into the void almost defying God not to answer and eventually we have come out of the other side. It reminds me in a way of my marriage vows; that even in dark days, in remaining faithful to them we have come through. That commitment to keep talking, even though it may feel as though nothing of much immediate significance is being said, is vital.

As my sight grew worse traditional types of daily prayer became more and more difficult. When readings, psalms and the main liturgy are all in different parts of the book and you have to flick from section to section using those fiddly little ribbon bookmarks, when type is small and printed on paper so thin you can see the letters from the other side drifting through, traditional forms of devotional practice and service books become inaccessible.

At the same time this was happening I began to talk to other disabled friends, people with a wide range of disabilities, and it became clear to me that there was a need for a form of daily prayer that was far simpler than what had gone before. Something much simpler in both structure and language. This Office would have to help those feeling estranged from church feel more connected to something bigger. It would have to help alleviate some of those feelings of isolation, of being cut off from the wider church.

Slowly I began to imagine creating prayers that were simple and accessible, prayers that honestly reflected our lives as twenty-first century disabled Christians here in the UK; being honest about all the beauty, the joy and even sometimes the anger and pain. I knew that nothing should be off the table. God wanted to hear it all; the good, the bad and the ugly.

I felt called to be writing prayers for those who were alone, isolated and estranged from the wider church. Prayers for those who suffer physical pain, prayers for those who struggled with issues of mental health, prayers for those whose experience of church had left them damaged in all kinds of ways. Prayers that conveyed hurt and anger as well as joy and hope.

In July 2018, The Ordinary Office went live at www.anordinaryoffice.co.uk and by the time we were a year old more than fifteen-hundred people a day were joining us in saying it. Our community was largely based in the UK but, many also joined us from around the globe. In July 2019 we led a service of morning prayer at the General Synod of the Church of England using The Ordinary Office, and for us it felt as if we had come of age. Finally the church was listening to the voices of those who felt dispossessed.

It always was, and indeed still is, my intention that this be an online resource. Our home is online, that is the place where we are seeking to build community. That said, I have been amazed at the number of people asking for some form of hard copy they could physically own, to treasure and hold. So, after much praying, waiting, searching and struggle, here it is, I hope that even in some small way it blesses you.

As I have said, this was created as and remains chiefly an online resource. By being part of the online experience you are able to pray alongside others, hopefully giving you a feeling you are a part of something bigger even though you well may be on your own.

So you are in your place and I in mine, but strangely through these prayers we somehow are 'alone together'. Strangely bound across time and space.

Almost like delving into a mystery …

RHYTHM

So many exiled people live lives of segregation, isolation and loneliness. A lack of punctuation, of rhythm, of clearly defined spaces of rest, work and prayer that were the very cornerstone of ancient monastic life are absent for so many of us, causing us to drift and to feel a disconnect deep in our soul.

For many, days are simply long monotonous spaces, to be endured rather than enjoyed and to be got through rather than fulfilled. Days to be endured rather than lived.

For us, a major part in this is the lack of such a rhythm of prayer.

A regular rhythm of prayer throughout the day gives it a structure and meaning that is not only good for the soul but nourishing to good mental health.

Rebecca says:
Rhythm is inherent in all of us. The first awareness we have is of our mother's heartbeat and breathing as we rest in the womb. We are born with inherent musicality, and it is the last sense we lose to diseases such as Dementia. To embrace a rhythm of prayer is to embrace life.

A FRESH EXPRESSION

St. Benedict's model of monastic life revolves around prayer, work, and life according to The Rule. The Rule is what brings rhythm and structure to the day.

For anyone wanting to help bring structure back to the day, this rhythm of prayer can be a huge help in this area.

This function has traditionally been fulfilled by the use of a breviary. The traditional breviary, however, is very difficult to use as it requires a lot of jumping about from section to section. It also changes according to the seasons.

Many disabled people need a liturgy that largely stays the same, making it easier to navigate. A liturgy that would become familiar and fixed in the memory. That people can relax into because they know what is coming, there will be no surprises. Peace is guaranteed.

For those of you who like to talk of fresh expressions and of pioneering, yes, this may seem like something new, but really it is simply a twenty-first century approach to the ancient monastic rhythm of the day. We hope it blesses you even just in a small way.

THE LANGUAGE OF INCLUSION

The secular world of equality, inclusion and diversity places great value on these terms and insists that to use them with any kind of claim to ownership carries a heavy price.

It is our belief that church has simply failed to grasp the value of such words out of a desire to be seen to be doing the right thing with little appreciation of the cost.

Let us try to explain. We all have preferred forms of liturgy and translations of scripture, forms that appeal to our individual sense of the aesthetic. This is our right and in certain circumstances it is perfectly correct. We ourselves (Dave and Rebecca) have certain preferences for styles of worship that may not speak to others as much as they do to us – and they are very different between the two of us. However, when it comes to our communal worship, we have a duty to make that as accessible to as many as possible in the first instance.

We need to consider our buildings, their sound and lighting, the music, the language and a host of other things. We must be prepared to set aside our own very personal preferences to achieve anything remotely accessible to all.

We love to use those words like 'inclusive, equal, diverse' and phrases like 'everyone welcome' but if significant numbers cannot access the building, read or understand the material, tolerate music that is too loud or over stimulating, understand language that is too academic, then they are left out and we can therefore not truthfully lay claim to those words and phrases. Believe me (Dave) when I tell you the secular world of disability will hold us accountable for that, as indeed many of my disabled friends have. Sadly, to date I feel all I can do is to hold my hands up and acknowledge that they are right.

These are some of the issues we are trying to address, and even as we write this, we know there will be ways in which we have failed – for which we are very sorry. But we need to start somewhere, and we need to know that we have played our part in moving things forward even just a little.

INCLUSIVE LANGUAGE – HE, SHE OR THEY?

Dave here:

It is important to recognise we are all products of our environment, and these things are so deep in our subconscious that things we say which have specific meaning to someone raised in the same environment can mean something radically different to someone outside that environment.

Let me try to explain by defining the criteria that make up my own environment. First of all, I was born in 1960, so I am a baby boomer. I am a Geordie with working class roots from a staunchly Labour heritage. I was raised a Roman Catholic, went to RC schools and did not mix with non-RC people until I started work at seventeen. I am a musician, a guitarist who grew up playing in rock bands on the North East club circuit in the late '70s to mid '80s.

Most of my oldest friends come from entirely similar backgrounds and so the language we use with each other has become a kind of shorthand. Short, staccato sentences that sound harsh to an outsider can mean something entirely different to an insider.

My oldest pal Colin and I grew up together through the same school, same church, same bands; we drank in the same pubs, went out with girls from the same group etc. As a result there developed a chemistry between us which was often unspoken, and when spoken could be completely misunderstood by strangers.

Because of our shared heritage, love and friendship when playing music together, if one of us was playing something the other didn't like they would be told, "That's f*&%ing crap!" Neither of us took offence, neither of us for one moment thought the other was calling in to question the other's musicianship, we were simply expressing our preference and that was mutually understood.

As I grew older, I started to play with musicians who did not share all these things in common and when I told them what they were playing was "f*&%ing crap" all kinds of trouble ensued. Egos were bruised, feelings hurt, tantrums were thrown and bands split up. It took me some time to understand why.

Inclusive language is like this. What has become acceptable shorthand between friends and peers has to be rethought to take regard of the sensitivities of others.

Rebecca says:
God is a he, right? Well, actually, God is genderless. God is God. God's gender is expressed through patriarchal human societies who present them as male because it reinforces the agenda that men are at the top of the pole. But God is beyond all human constructs, therefore God is beyond gender. Jesus had a male

body, yet Jesus is one aspect of God, not God in their entirety.

You may be a little confused by my use of Them/Their to address God. Dave continues to use He/Him. I prefer plural pronouns. This in no way denies the one-ness of God. One of the many gifts of Queer Theology is the ability to understand personhood in a non-binary way.

Once I decided addressing God exclusively as He/Him no longer worked for me, I tried out She/Her, but in many ways that felt equally problematic. I feel deeply spiritually nourished in exploring the feminine divine and learning more about that aspect of God, but I don't feel comfortable engaging directly with God in that way. Once I took the step towards removing binary gender from the equation altogether and embracing They/Them, I immediately felt at peace with that decision and have used those pronouns ever since. He or She only addresses one aspect of who God is. They allows for all.

I don't for one moment expect everyone to feel comfortable with this immediately. Dave and I have discussed what to use throughout this book, and our decision has been to each use our own preferred pronouns for God, alongside including this chapter exploring the issue. We aim to inform discussion, not dictate what you should or shouldn't do. But we hope to have given you food for thought.

Dave again:

I know deep in my heart that the pronouns Rebecca uses are the right ones, but equally I am a product of my generation. When I hear myself using the same pronouns as Rebecca, even though I know she is right, I hear myself and to me I sound like some sad old bloke trying to use modern parlance to be 'down with the kids' and it makes me embarrassed, like watching someone dad dance. So I will stick with my old way, not because I neither know nor care but simply because I am a self-conscious old fool. In this, I ask for your understanding and forgiveness.

Rebecca says:

Awareness is step one. We all have to deconstruct before we can rebuild with a more intentional outlook, and it is never a comfortable place to be. This is why conversations are vital, and in having them – as we are here on paper - change can be nurtured. That is my greatest hope for this chapter, and indeed this book.

THOUGHTS ON ONLINE CHURCH

Many of us that are exploring ideas of online church have arrived here not because we have deliberately chosen to leave traditional forms of church, but rather because we feel such churches have abandoned us.

We are trying to imagine what it is to be a Christian when we have been abandoned by the official brands of Christianity, left to find a faith life outside of church. Of course, our overall goal is to pray for change in the Church, change that would eventually lead to us being welcomed back home, but for many of us the question is where do we go in the meantime? How do we find a place that is safe and welcoming for us to be right now?

Much of our thinking in recent years would seem to have much in common with the 'radical theology' of Pete Rollins and others, but whereas they seem to have reached their position through thought and study, we seem to have arrived here by accident, through a feeling of rejection by the ordinary church.

There is a feeling that mainstream church regards those exiled groups of people as in some way less, a feeling that when they set out to create an expression of church that meets their needs it is then rubbished by the very church that is failing them.

It was never our deliberate intention to become an online expression of Church. Our presence online has simply grown out of necessity. More and more we have come to recognise that disabled people unable to access on-site church, and other disenfranchised groups, were using online as a way of gathering together in ways that simply were not possible for them in an on-site space. In the words of Peter, 'Lord, to whom shall we go? You have the words of eternal life. We believe and know that you are the Holy One of God.' (John 6:68-69, NIV).

So much of the focus of traditional church organisations when it comes to the online world is on how to convert those online followers into on-site church members in our pews (bums on seats).

This attitude, we believe, has led to many problems. The biggest one is that too often online has been seen as a lazy option for those who simply can't be bothered to get out of bed on a Sunday morning.

It has been seen as letting such people off the hook. It has been seen as a lesser expression of church by a church that is failing people, yet is still critical when those that it is failing create something for themselves that actually meets their needs. This would seem like wanting it both ways.

The vision of online church which God has been revealing to me (Dave) has an entirely different focus. The people who are gathering around us may never ever translate into on-site members of any church. The buildings and services offered by on-site church simply do not serve them. The way traditional church is structured seems in many ways to mitigate against a truly successful expression of church.

Online is truly global and will simply grow where it will. It cannot be managed or restricted to a parish, deanery or diocese, yet alone a denomination or nation. Traditional church struggles with this concept because they don't hold the power, they cannot control it.

We tend to organise projects within those traditional structures and whichever parish, deanery, diocese or denomination sets up the project expects to be able to calculate some tangible return for its own organisation.

For us this seems to completely miss the point. Online church is so completely a work of the Holy Spirit and will blow where it will; because of that traditional structures simply cannot manage or contain it. If we are setting up an online church project simply to convert that into extra bums on our pews it will not work.

The Ordinary Office project is online simply to serve those that gather there, it has no agenda as to bringing those people back into some on-site space that we own or control. Should it lead to people returning to church we would be more than happy but that is NOT why we are here. That choice is for those we empower to make, not us to dictate.

TRAUMA

Please read this chapter with care, or skip ahead to p.89 should you need to.

Rebecca says:
How many times have we heard it said that something traumatised someone? Perhaps their child played a prank on them which made them jump. Or perhaps their favourite character died in a TV series.

Or perhaps they were a victim of abuse within their church.

Many of you reading this book will fall under this latter category. From having your gifts and callings stifled due to your sexuality or theology, to having been mentally, spiritually or physically abused. The spectrum is vast, and the harm is deep.

Yet we as victims are seen as backsliders, faithless, when we flee in great pain from the places we love but can no longer bear to be within. From the people we care about but uphold the structures who harm us. From the relationships we have nurtured but now don't know if we can maintain.

The wrenching, tearing pain experienced when leaving a church family is unspeakable. When it goes unnoticed by many, it is lonely. When it is followed by rumour, gossip and shaming, the experience is a traumatic one.

The Church is responsible for so much trauma amongst the flock it is meant to protect. Yet the expectation is we are to remain within it, keep taking the blows, while the institution stands firm. Unyielding. To say change moves at a snail's pace would be generous. We cannot stay, yet when we go and find our freedom and peace in the wilderness, we are deemed dangerous. Heathen. Unchurched.

My siblings, I dance in the wilderness with joy. Because here is where I am closest to God. Here I find church in diverse nature, in diverse people, in diverse theologies, in diverse thinking. I can think for myself, breathe in deeply, be made whole. In the wilderness, I am no longer a slave to another man's interpretation of how I must believe, but I am free to believe in the God who speaks to my heart. I am free to reject theology which harms and embrace theology which loves. I can heal.

Many things in my life have truly traumatised me. I know what trauma means. Divorce. Sexual Assault. Domestic Violence. Church traumatised me. Being in the wilderness with God and their church healed me.

Dave says:
It is being left to people outside The Church to sort out the mess it has made, and it is being left to those people to fund the work as well. The Church needs to fund a separate body, so it is independent, which can then support us.

They made the mess; they should pay for it. Its reparations for the harm they have caused. But they can't be involved in the work to support people because they caused the harm.

It's like an abusive relationship. You wouldn't ask an escaped victim to go back into the relationship without having first been supported and the abuser having done some work to make changes. I'm not saying people should never go back. But there's an awful lot of work to be done first.

If you have found anything in this chapter challenging or triggering, please do reach out to your support networks, local or on-line support networks or any of the organisations listed at the back of this book.

You are not alone and there are helpers available.

Peace be with you.

CHOICES

We all make choices about every aspect of church life that may well have unintended consequences for someone else's accessibility needs.

The type of liturgy that we prefer may well use language that is simply too complex for people with certain disabilities. The decor we choose for our buildings may cause others problems with physical access. Our style of worship music may be too loud for some.

Every decision we make involves a level of trade off in someone else's level of accessibility: we must learn to be sensitive to this and not just dismiss voices of concern.

We cannot casually throw around phrases like 'everyone welcome' or words like 'inclusion' or 'equality' without being aware of what impact our choices are having on these words and phrases for others.

During COVID-19 we casually threw around the expression 'all in it together' but as we began to unlock many were left feeling abandoned and wondering just what happened to all in this together?

In writing for The Ordinary Office we are aware there have been such trade offs in trying to produce liturgies that are simple and easy to understand, yet retain enough elements of the poetic to appeal and provide the beauty we believe worship should contain.

We would dare to suggest that for us this is as accessible as we can make our work whilst still retaining enough of the artistic credentials that we both hold dear, and that we require to meet these thresholds. In doing so we are sure we will have made some mistakes that mean we have compromised someone else's accessibility. There will always be this tension; we can strive to minimise it, but we can never erase it.

We are sad about that but truly believe this is a tension we all have to grapple with, and this is by no means a one size fits all solution. If one even exists.

We name our discomfort and limitations, and we invite discussion about it. We reflect together weekly, at times even daily, on our work. We actively invite contributions, and we are always open to feedback. In this way we hold the space for inclusive practice and strive to ensure it means inclusive. Where we fail, we are truly sorry. But we also invite you to learn from what we do get right, celebrate where Jesus has blessed us and walk onwards with us as we continue to learn ourselves.

SACRAMENTS

Rebecca says:

There is much debate about whether we can receive sacraments, in particular the Eucharist, online. Dave and I held back from including Communion in our services for a long time, even though we have very much wanted to.

Yet in 2022, we made the decision to take the step and address the issue. We'd like to share our journey on this with you now.

I will note, this is very much from a Protestant position, with the two sacraments of Communion and Baptism focused on. I understand the Catholic position is more complex, but I am approaching these issues very much from a Protestant approach. It is useful to make this clear at the outset.

When I was growing up, Communion for me was a bread bun from the local baker, McRaes, and a cup of Ribena. We were a Free Church, non-denominational, and that Communion was no less meaningful or transformational to me than the Anglican Eucharist I received at the altar twenty years later. I have experienced both. I understand both.

From the hands of my lay minister and from the hands of an ordained Bishop, wafer or white loaf, alcohol or no, the meaning was in the experience and my relationship with God. I absolutely stay by the assertion that the physical items, the substances, whose hands blessed them, who placed them in my hands, the room I was in, who I was with, none of those things were vital to the sacramental experience. What happened between God and I, the inward blessing of Grace and the outward expression of that, was what mattered.

So, why can that not happen online? Are we limiting God in such a way that we say if the blessing or prayer is said over a microphone and transmitted into another room they can't work through that anymore? That dilutes God's power? That if the bread and wine is seeded loaf and fruit juice from the kitchen cupboard,

It becomes unusable in God's eyes? That if my hands are the only hands that touch the items, God cannot use them? That if the community witnessing the outward act of grace is dispersed, and the sense of place and time is not linear, God can't work with that? I think not.

The Bible is full of God taking scenarios and making sacraments out of the ordinary. Philip baptised the Ethiopian Eunuch in a puddle. He didn't say 'No, we must wait until there is a crowd of witnesses and Holy Water'. He acted there and then, because God was with them. Acts 2:46 tells us the early Jesus-followers met in the temple but shared bread in their home. It doesn't tell us the apostles were praying over the bread and blessing it before solemnly passing it out, we are told 'in the houses they were breaking loaves of bread, and they were receiving food as they celebrated'

(ABPE). They were sharing a meal and celebrating Jesus as they did so.

The Church has taken every day ordinary yet extra-ordinary Graces and turned them into something elitist, ableist, that can only be accessed at certain times when a service is on, or when a priest can visit you. What about care home residents, those in hospital, those of us with chronic illnesses unable to get to churches and without an active attachment to a site?

We need online sacraments.

It is worth noting here the meaning of what a sacrament is has changed over the years, and varies between church traditions. The seven Catholic sacraments weren't consolidated until the Second Council of Lyon in 1274, while the Eastern Orthodox Church acknowledge there are special sacraments but considers everything the church does as church to be sacramental.

3rd century Christian writer Tertullian referred to sacraments as the equivalent of a Roman Soldier's Oath of Allegiance, named the same. The definition we commonly use today is accredited to Augustine of Hippo in the 5th Century. I always plead with anyone saying there is only one way, there has never only been one way. Were the early Christians sharing Communion doing it wrong because it didn't fit with the Book of Common Prayer?

In 1 Peter 2, those who follow Jesus are described as 'a holy priesthood' (v.5, NIV) and later in the same chapter 'a royal priesthood' (v.9). Martin Luther uses these verses, along with Revelation 5:10, to underpin one of the foundational principles of Protestantism, declaring 'we are all consecrated priests through Baptism' (Rupp & Drewery, 1970). This view, that we all have direct access to God, and therefore are able to access the grace brought to us through the sacraments directly, empowers us to champion online sacraments. We have a biblical stance, as it were.

I, as a member of the holy priesthood, in my own home, alongside others doing the same, can access the grace of God directly, and engage in the outward sign of this through bread and wine, or sprinkling of water. The only reason to deny a person this, if they are understanding, consenting and requesting, is rooted in ableism and elitism.

Dave says:

It is 11 am on a sunny Saturday morning in July 1967 and I am standing on the steps to St Augustine's RC Church in Felling on Tyneside. I'm dressed in grey, short trousers, a brilliant white shirt and bright red tie. My mother (also my primary teacher at this time) has me shining my shoes on the back of my socks as she spits onto her handkerchief and roughly scrubs at my chin. We are waiting to process into Mass to celebrate my first Holy Communion.

I remember this scene so vividly today at the age of sixty-two, I think, because it is the first memory I have of a feeling of awe. I knew deep in my seven-year-old heart I was about to take part in something wonderful, something otherworldly. I could not explain its significance, I doubt I could today some fifty-five years later. But it was a tangible feeling that I remember to this day; a feeling that on the darkest of days when God seems a million miles away, even on days when God seems to not exist at all, I can still summon up and it sustains me.

This feeling keeps me tied into my relationship with Jesus, a relationship that in those intervening years has often been painful and sometimes very distant. It is part of my belief that God grants us spiritual highlights so that we may cling to them in dark times. This one was right up there with them despite my tender age and lack of understanding.

All through my school days I had a deep feeling of Jesus walking with me. I had been a premature baby with many health issues, and between birth and my teens underwent many operations spending long periods in hospital. When I was four, my mother was told by surgeons to simply take me home and love me, as I probably would not survive much longer. Because of this my parents and grandparents kept me tightly cosseted and were more than reluctant to let me join with the other lads playing football, british bulldog or snowball fighting in winter.

I remember one winter's day after I had just come home from surgery, I could hear the other boys playing outside in the snow but could not join in. My grandad put two sheets of plywood on the kitchen floor and brought six wheelbarrow loads of snow into my grandmother's kitchen so that I too could build a snowman. My grandmother's response to Grandad was to ask why he couldn't have built me a snowman in the garden where I could have watched from the window. I can still hear Grandad's booming Geordie voice saying "Now then Mary! That bairn can hear all his pals playing and he wants to be part of it. How would he be part of it watching me, a daft old get, building it for him?" Grandad knew the true meaning of equality. He knew that it meant feeling as included as possible.

All through this period I fought against this excessive cosseting. I knew I was unwell but I also knew I was in Jesus' care; the Jesus that came to me in my first Holy Communion.

In early 1983 I left the RC seminary, already an ordained deacon, literally only a few weeks away from full ordination. I had reported abuse being committed by clergy within my order to the principal of the order, and for my trouble he threw me out. But it didn't end there.

I left the seminary in the January. In July of that same year, I met the girl I have now been married to for thirty-five years.

By August, my former order was putting it about that I had been carrying on a secret affair with her and that was why I had left.

For the next two years I stayed away from all forms of church as I was so hurt. Yet in 1985 I was persuaded to join my pals Andy Raine & John Skinner (co-founders of what became the Northumbria Community) on Holy Island for an Easter workshop.

On Easter Sunday morning I found myself on the tiny Cuthbert Island just off the shores of Lindisfarne for a sunrise Eucharist. When it came to the Eucharistic Prayer, John, a vicar who knew the hurt I was carrying, invited me to join him at our makeshift altar and to say the Eucharistic Prayer. This was a huge healing gift for me and I cried my way through the rest of that service.

What I'm trying to show by telling you all of this is that, for me, Eucharist is an inclusive, all-encompassing thing which includes a sense of belonging to something far bigger. The things I see about Reserved Sacrament, Eucharistic ministers taking Communion to the sick etc., these just don't cut it. We need to feel part of the whole service. Being present at the Consecration is every bit as important to us as receiving the bread and wine.

Here in 2022, I find myself leading an online community of more than almost twenty-thousand, The Ordinary Office being said online more than eight-thousand times a day and an average of one-hundred people a week watching our Sunday service at the time of writing. This community is made up of many who feel disenfranchised from mainstream church, because of issues of disability, race, ethnicity, sexuality, gender and other forms of discrimination; sometimes people are carrying with them trauma from abuse, physical, emotional and spiritual. Many of these people have been so damaged by church that they find themselves unable to attend. For them church is no longer a safe space, yet they long to take part in the Eucharist. They are being failed twice by The Church; firstly by the way they have been abused and forced out, then secondly by their desire to have some form of online

Eucharist and having The Church declare it invalid.

When the priest raises the Host at the consecration, do the back doors of the Church burst open and does the risen Jesus march smartly down the aisle? No! Yet is Jesus present? Yes! So if he doesn't have to be in the room to be present where is the problem?

Rebecca says:
We know only too well this is a challenge to orthodoxy, which is why we have taken time to consider our stance carefully. But more and more, as on-site spaces are opening back up and traditional Eucharistic practices are available to those who believe that is the only, correct

way to receive, our vulnerable siblings are left behind.

So while we expand Christian practices to be more inclusive, as the Jewish Jesus followers did in accepting Gentiles to the group, we pray for grace from those who don't agree with our methods. That you may see our heart is to serve God and bring their people closer to them. And that we truly believe they will honour our intent, knowing our hearts are faithful.

Peace be with you.

Here in the middle of the day, I take a moment, pause and pray

PRAYERS FOR HOLY DAYS AND HIGH DAYS

ASH WEDNESDAY

Lord. We are here to confess that we have fallen short.

We come to admit that without your mercy we would simply be dust.

Stay close to us through this Lenten season and truly free us from all temptation.

We hope for Easter and the promise that death has no sting.

We offer you all glory, all honour and all praise.

Although formed only from dust our spirits cry out for your redemption.

Amen.

PALM SUNDAY

What a contradiction. The King is coming, we shout. Hosanna in the highest, we call. Yet we fail to understand that you are the Servant King, the King who washes his disciples' feet, who came not with an army but with a boundless love. A love that would take you to the cross.

Lord, as we sing 'Hosanna' today, may you remind us where this road leads.

Help us to place our lives before you, to let us be Your servants too.

Amen.

MAUNDY THURSDAY

On that last night in that upper room
He washed his disciples' feet.
He handed his life back to you.
He knew full well what was ahead
And what did he do?

He knelt down on the floor,
And washed his friends' feet.

He was their teacher and their Lord,

Yet he washed their feet.

Teach us to do likewise.
Glory to him who serves.

Amen.

GOOD FRIDAY

Lord, as you were crucified between two thieves, one who ridiculed you and one who repented, let our feeble lives and the disabilities we carry be a witness to the scope of your love and a demonstration of true healing; not cure but healing.

Lord, this seems such a short prayer on such a momentous day, but we are so in shock and awe that the only words we can really manage are:

Thank You. Thank You. Thank You.

Amen.

EASTER DAY

Your light is rising like the dawn.

Our hearts rejoice,

The night has gone.

The stone has been rolled away.

You come back, walk among us

And show us your wounds.

They did not disappear.

You have not been cured

But you conquered death

And promise us the same.

Amen.

PENTECOST

We ask you to send your Spirit among us
this day.

Grant us a new birth, that we may look
afresh, free from cynicism and jadedness.

Give us a new passion to our faith.
Help us as we recommit ourselves.
Grant us a courage we could not have
imagined.

Teach us to love as you have loved,
To give without counting the cost,
To set out in to the light unafraid.

Amen.

CHRISTMAS MORNING

Lord, you know what it means to be vulnerable. A fragile young life, a defenceless baby, born in a stable to parents who were far from home and very afraid.

Lord we are vulnerable too, we don't know what lies ahead.

Take our vulnerable hearts and draw them ever closer to you.

Amen.

EPIPHANY

God of light, a light that breaks through
the darkness.
A light that penetrates all hidden corners.

A light that come to us through a little
child, born in Bethlehem.

We have followed your star
And it has brought us here

May we continue to diligently search for
him each day
So that we may offer our lives to you
In joy and thanksgiving.

Amen.

Time to wind down, whether with family and friends, or simply alone with you.

PRAYERS FOR DIFFICULT SITUATIONS

*This section contains a range of prayers
written for particular situations
which have been well received on our
Twitter page.*

THE CARERS

Teach us a new song, Lord,

A song for those who go unsung.

Praise the ones who do our dirty work.

The pushers of chairs, the wipers of

bums,

The makers of tea, the givers of meds.

Teach us that new song, Lord,

That lets them know they are loved.

The ones who put their own dreams on

hold, Lord,

That give until they are spent.

The ones who go unnoticed, Lord,

Quietly meeting our needs

Yet keep us rolling along.

Teach us to say thank you, Lord,

For every ounce of care.

Amen.

FOR FRIENDS UNMET

For the Tweet that says I'm praying,

The hand across the sky.

The one whom I speak to every day

Yet whose face I've never seen.

The voice that soothes me when I'm troubled

Yet whose tone I'll never know.

For the friends I've made in cyberspace,

The friends who fill the void.

The family unrelated

Yet closer than they know.

I thank you, Lord,

For all of them

And place them in your care.

Amen.

TAKE THIS ANGER

Take all this bloody anger, Lord,

And chuck it in the bin.

Every last bit of spite and bile

That chokes away my breath.

Replace the cry that shouts, "Why me!"

With one that says, "Why not?"

And when the last bitter word is spent,

Fill that void with songs of praise to you.

Songs that say, 'Thank You', Lord,

For the hope that your love brings,

For all the care that is shown to me,

For the blood you so dearly spent.

Fill my heart with love instead

And teach me how to dance.

Amen.

BITTERNESS

Bitterness has sneaked in again.

A coldness in my bones.

It has stolen my joy

And filled my heart with spite.

Cast out this doubt, Lord.

Cast out all fear.

Help me to start over.

Teach me joy in small things.

A kind word,

A casual smile,

A joke to raise a laugh.

Replace all hate with kindness, Lord,

Teach me what it means to repent.

Amen.

WHEN SUNDAY COMES AROUND

Sunday has come around again,
And all over the land
Church doors are opening.
Musicians are tuning instruments,
Altar cloths placed on tables,
Candles lit, Vestments put on.

And here I am God, alone!
So many churches do not meet my
needs.
I cannot climb the stairs,
I cannot hear the celebrant,
The language is too complex,
I cannot read the literature.
I have been so hurt by bad Bible teaching
I simply cannot face it again.

Yet for all that, I miss it. I need to feel part of something, something much bigger than me. Part of the wider body of Christ.

So I come to this online place, a place where so many of us gather. Alone, and yet strangely together. We come with our loneliness, our brokenness, our feelings of being cut off, cast adrift. Yet we find much comfort in this place as we build this online community, an expression of your eternal love.

So we offer all this back to you, God, as our gift to your wider church. Out of our broken lives we say to your Sunday Church: come, see where we live, share our pilgrim journey, travel with us, share this road. We may not be able to access your place, but instead be assured of a welcome in ours.

You can lean on us as we lean on you.

This Sunday we pray for your whole church; the seen and the invisible, those who are gathered and those who are scattered. Unite us all in a spirit of community.

Bring your broken body back together; not cured, but broken, yet healed.

Amen.

CAN'T PRAY

Today I cannot pray.

There are no words.

I feel no hope, I am broken.

I am alone!

God, I feel estranged from you.
Today you seem hidden from me.
Your voice is out of reach.

I stretch out my hand but cannot reach
your hand.

I cry out but my voice echoes back in the
darkness; there is no answer.

I am alone on this mountainside with the howl of the wind and the cry of the wild wolf.

I am alone.

But I shall wait for your voice knowing that it will come as it always has before.

For now, I shall borrow this prayer until once again I am able to pray in my own words.

Amen.

LONELINESS

Lord, it is just too much today.

The room is too empty,

The silence is too long.

The sound of my own voice is not

enough.

Answer me when I call.

Talk to me when I feel alone.

Lord, it was you who said

When two or three are gathered

There I am in the midst of them.

Gather us together now,

Be it on-site or on-line,

And enter into the midst of us.

Touch us with your presence.

Warm us with your love.

Amen.

GATHER US TOGETHER

Though we are scattered, Lord,
Gather us together.

Though we are alone, Lord,
Unite us in prayer.

Though we are far apart,
Let us feel a closeness.

Let us reach out across the ether
As hands across the sea.

We are in your temple, Lord,
Although there are no walls.

The web is where we gather,
As real as any church.

Computers, phones and tablets are our
prayer books.
These strangers are my friends.

Mark this as holy ground,
A virtual sacred space.

Amen.

JOURNEY

Staggering, stumbling,

Lurching, limping,

Whatever the way.

Crawling, walking,

Falling and then rising,

Whatever the way.

On stretchers, in wheelchairs,

With canes and with guide dogs,

Whatever the way.

With crutches and sticks,

Arm in arm, hand in hand,

Whatever the way.

I'll carry you if you'll carry me,
We'll carry each other,
Forward together,
Whatever the way.

Amen.

MARKING THE WAY

God of our fathers, support us as we take
on this work of building a waymark to you.

May this work help to create an open,
inclusive, accessible and welcoming
church as we carry your word with us like
stones.

As we make this pilgrim journey, help us
make note of those who call out to you.
Help us pay attention to the people in our
community with disabilities, to take the
time to listen as they communicate their
needs, desires and prayers in whatever
way is open to them.

Help us to build partnerships, to remain mindful of our limitations and continue the journey even when we feel like giving in.

May we continue to be part of a community that values the gifts of each other, while respecting the varying challenges that each of us faces.

Guide us as we work to create space where each unique person feels comfortable and seen, where difference is viewed as a blessing.

And as we journey, let us place these stones we carry as cairns to mark the way for those that follow after.

Amen.

WHAT MEAN THESE STONES?

Each carries a stone inscribed with his
word.
He is our traveling companion,
Our mountain guide.
He is the way.

No journey plan,
No fixed destination,
No planned stops along the way.
Where he leads is not our concern.

Walking in faith
With God as our guide,
Resting where he lays us down.

Rising refreshed with the sun,

Starting each day with enthusiasm,

Sharing the bread and wine He gives.

Trusting in him,

Trusting in one another,

Sharing the road, the load and the
journey.

Arriving safely at his destination,

Knowing we are where we should be,

We place our stones in this sacred cairn.

Amen.

LOGO

Write it on our hearts, Lord,

In letters bright and bold.

A logo that says 'Made in Heaven,

Copyright Jesus the Lord.'

Write it in ink that will not fade.

Write it in braille and symbols too.

Write it for everyone,

Leave no one out.

Let ALL Your people know.

Tell them they are precious,

Tell them they are yours.

One family, equal and true.

One people, one body,

Made in the image of You.

Amen.

THE GOD OF GOOGLE

You keep no record.

You write no snarky post.

You don't post it on YouTube.

No trolling for you.

You take all our failings,

Our darkest of secrets,

And you say they are over.

You say they are gone.

They cannot be Googled.

They are not lurking in cyberspace

Waiting to pounce.

You say let us start over.

Tomorrow is a new day.

No judgment, no hate, no bitterness, no grudge.

It is so easy to say sorry

Although so hard to forgive.

Yet you do it so willingly.

Forgive all of us, Lord,

Even though we do not easily forgive.

Amen.

HOSPITAL AT NIGHT

Lying in a strange bed

Listening to the snoring of strangers,

The beeps of strange machines,

Worrying about my future.

Missing loved ones,

Stressed and in pain,

I place my trust in you.

As I face another night

Missing home,

Alone and afraid,

Grant me rest.

Grant me peace.

Grant me healing.

And above all else grant me hope.

Amen.

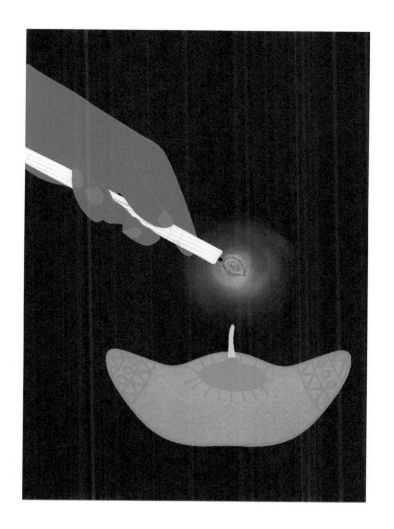

Lamplighter! Lover, friend. You are the keeper of my dreams.

THE
DAILY OFFICE

AN INTRODUCTION TO MORNING PRAYER

Oh, that we could just throw back the covers and leap out of bed to greet the day with boundless enthusiasm! Sadly, for many disabled people this is only a dream. Mornings are difficult.

Perhaps we have to wait for the arrival of a carer to get us up - a carer that arrives at a time of their convenience, not ours.

There is medication to take and many of us have to wait till these meds kick in and our bodies adjust before our day begins.

The gap between getting up and going out to face the world can be a long one, if indeed we are able to go out and face the world at all. If, indeed, we have anything to get up and go out for.

But just for this morning, Lord, we are going to say these words with you.

MORNING PRAYER

We praise you, Lord, because we are ALL
fearfully and wonderfully made.
In our Father's house there is room for all;
there are no rejects.

There are no able-bodied, there are no
disabled.
There are only his beloved children
who are all made in his image.
We are all beautiful in his eyes.

We believe Jesus himself ascended into
heaven,
carrying his wounds on our behalf.
Jesus does not hide these wounds.

They carry no shame for him, he shows them to us willingly as proof of his eternal love.

He calls us this morning to do the same, to stand before him in our brokenness, trusting in him for our care.

I hear footsteps in the garden and I know my Lord is near. He calls me by my name saying, "Why are you hiding from me? Why are you hiding from me? Why do you hide from me when I love you so?"

Those who cannot see he walks along side as our guide.

He whispers softly to those who cannot hear.

He soothes those whose minds are troubled.

He rides with those who cannot walk.

He sees the pain of those whose pain cannot be seen and brings insight to those who appear not to understand.

He is at the heart of every lonely room and is present in every stranger who sits at our hearth.

His love is new every morning.
His love does not depend on our fragile form.
His love is enough for this coming day.

We accept the calling to bring that love to those we meet today.

Lord, when I hear you calling, help me to say, "Here I am."

Only you can meet the longing of my heart.
Only you knows every hidden part.

Show me the gifts I have.
Show me the gift I am.

Let my whole life be lived in love of you,
Bringing great joy to your heart.

Amen.

AN INTRODUCTION TO MID-DAY PRAYER

By now many of us will need more care. Maybe someone to help us with toileting, to administer drugs, to rearrange us in our beds, to prepare lunch, or to actually feed us. This can be a time of day that simply reminds us of how much we are reliant on the care of others.

More than anything, Lord, we rely on your care. So we turn to you this lunchtime.

MID-DAY PRAYER

Here in the middle of the day

I take a moment, pause and pray.

Each breath you give me, God,

You know my heart,

and know its every beat.

You are closer to me than breathing,

nearer than hands or feet.

I matter to you more than many sparrows.

You catch each word I frame.

You care about my day,

design new patterns with my name.

If the day seems dull and empty,

I will gather it to you.

If the day is long and busy,

still I return to you.

Amen.

AN INTRODUCTION TO EVENING PRAYER

For many of us, early evening is when the care system kicks back in. People come to change us, to make us comfortable, to dispense our meds or to prepare our food.

Often this may be the only contact we have had in a long day. We look forward to it not just because of all these practical things but as the chance to see a friendly face, to hear a friendly voice, to feel a human touch.

EVENING PRAYER

Lord, as evening approaches
Grant us time to relax.
A chance to review our day.

Time to wind down
Whether with family and friends
Or simply alone with you.

Even if the only company we have had
today has been that of those we have
shared prayer with online,
We thank you for bringing us through this
day
And we join with all the others of this
community.
Alone, yet together.

Be with us this evening as we converse
with them
In our home that is on Twitter.

Amen.

AN INTRODUCTION TO NIGHT PRAYER

This is the time that many of us fear the most. So many of us live alone, the carers are all gone and we face long hours to ourselves.

We earnestly pray for a peaceful night, that sleep will come, and pain and nightmares be banished.

NIGHT PRAYER

Lord, I know you carry a torch for me,
and I am fearfully and wonderfully made.
Deep in the darkest night you love me
in all my uniqueness,
and you are the keeper of my dreams.

When my thoughts come too fast
and trouble me, soothe me into rest.

When I get caught in the loop,
gently get me free again.
You ease the weight of my being.

You even know just when to interrupt
this night-time conversation and say,
'Hush, enough now,
let's talk about it in the morning...'

Even in the dark of night,

You leave a light on for me,

and are always watching over me.

Lamplighter! Lover, friend.

You are the keeper of my dreams.

Be mine this night.

Amen.

NOCTURNE

For the nights we have trouble sleeping.

Lord, the Bogeyman is here again.

Stealing away our rest,

Haunting our dreams,

Playing with our fears

In the wee small hours.

When our monsters stalk the corridors of

our minds,

Wading through the backwaters of our

day,

And our pain, anxiety and worries run riot.

When our medication is not working.

When the only voice we hear

Is the echo of our own doubt

Laughing at our fragile faith,

Shaking the foundations of our belief.

Wake from your sleep at the back of the
boat, dear Jesus, and calm the waters.
Quell the storm that engulfs us and bring
your calm, your peace, your rest.

When our feeble faith deserts us and fear
runs amok, lend us yours.
We know that will be enough
As it has been so many times before.

Let nothing cause us to fear, to send us
running.
Let no concern overwhelm us.
Let all pain be dulled,
All nerves be calm.
Take us gently back in to sleep,
Watching over us 'til dawn's light.

As we click the AMEN button

Let us watch others do the same

And know we are not alone.

Somewhere in the night

Another calls your name.

Amen.

Take us gently back in to sleep, watching
over us 'til dawn's light

EXTRA
MATERIAL

Here you will find graces, liturgy and choices of blessings that you may wish to add to your Daily Office prayers.

LITURGY FOR ONLINE COMMUNION

PREFACE

Let us take a moment to pause, gather our thoughts and focus our minds on this space, this time, this place.

Whether joining this Communion at a time we know others are too, or at a time of our own choosing, let us take a moment to recognise the Spirit within us constantly unites us to those around us, Jesus Christ and the God of all.

We are never truly alone, always apart together. With the recognition of this truth, we enter into this sacred act of shared Communion now.

PRAYER OF HUMBLE ACCESS

God of all pilgrims, who meets us as we are, we ask to join with you today.

We know of our own accord we have no right to ask, yet by your grace we have been given every right.

We know in our own weakness we haven't the strength to access, yet by your power we have all the strength we need.

We know by our own confession we are not worthy, yet by your forgiveness we have become worth everything and more.

Take us, your humble children, God, and bless us with the knowledge of your constant, never ending love, that we may come joyfully to you transformed as your holy priesthood. No longer ashamed and no longer afraid.

Amen.

PRAYER OF CONSECRATION

Holy Spirit, she who moves beyond time and space. She who binds us, unites us, gives us confidence in the living God. Come to us now, as we are, where we are, when we are.

She who was with Jesus on that day, when he broke the bread and said 'Take, eat. This is my body, which is given for you. Do this in remembrance of me.' Be with us as you were with Jesus that day, moving beyond the boundaries of time as the mystery allows.

She who was with Jesus on that day, when he took the cup and said 'Take, drink. This is my blood, which is shed for you. Do this in remembrance of me.' Be with us as you were with Jesus that day, moving beyond the boundaries of time as the mystery allows.

Amen.

ACT OF COMMUNION

We accept this bread in whatever form we take it, and recognise it as the body of Christ. We eat it, and remember him.

We accept this wine in whatever form we share it, and recognise it as the blood of Christ. We drink it, and remember him.

THE LORD'S PRAYER

PRAYER AFTER COMMUNION

God of all time and place, who dwells within us. We thank you for enabling this act of Communion in a way we can all take part in.

We thank you for being with us when no-one else can, and for drawing us into community with others who share the same circumstance.

Through the profound mystery of your ways, we can be blessed by your body and blood at a time and distance, apart yet together, in a way that we can only marvel at.

We accept this bread in whatever form we take it, and we accept this wine in whatever form we share it, as a sign of our covenant with you.

We love you, God who sustains, bonds and creates. Work within our hearts this day and always.

Amen.

PRAYER OF PRAISE

Lord of the Dance, Jesus Christ, our friend and fellow on the journey this day and always. We thank you for your continued commitment to our lives.

We are in awe of your faithfulness, your never-ending companionship, your dedication and your love.

We praise you for your sacrifice, which never fails us, and we thank you for reaching out to us across time and space regardless of how we meet – online, onsite or hybrid.

We invite you again and again into the centre of our hearts, Jesus, so we may be your hands, your voice, your presence in this world, beacons of hope and reflections of your love.

Amen.

BLESSING

May the refreshing breath of the Holy
Spirit blow through your life this day.

May the joyful companionship of Jesus be
present in your life this day.

May the all-surrounding love of God be
known fully to you this day.

May you know the care and fellowship of
your online community, valued and
cherished as you are, joined through
Wi-Fi, Communion and the mystery of the
Holy Trinity.

Peace and blessings be upon you, this
day and always.

Amen.

GRACES

BEFORE A MEAL

Thank you God for this simple meal.

Whether eaten alone or among friends,

It is enough to know that you provide for us.

May we be always willing to share what we have.

AFTER A MEAL

Thank you God for hungry bodies filled,

For needs taken care of

And the love of your provision.

Teach us to provide for others

As you have provided for us today.

ALTERNATIVE MORNING BLESSINGS

1.

This morning let it be enough.

Enough to be awake.

Enough to whisper "Jesus."

Enough to feel your presence

Like seeds floating in the air.

2.

Gone is the night. Gone is the fear.

Gone are the nightmares.

Hope rises with the dawn.

3.

Sun peeks through the curtains
Beckoning us to rise.
Let us throw wide the windows
And welcome in your dawn.

4.

Jesus is calling! Jesus is calling
'I have prepared a meal for you.
Let us breakfast on the beach.'

5.

Do not worry about the questions
Of where to sleep or where to eat.
My hands, like the sky, will hold you.
I will not let you fall.

6.

Wipe the sleep from your eyes.

Comb your bedtime hair.

Brush your teeth and face the dawn.

Set off with me into the light.

7.

Morning has broken,

It can't be mended.

God made it that way

To show night had ended.

8.

We are broken but not useless.

We are battered but not overwhelmed.

Because we know that you have blessed

us and in your love we will prevail.

9.

Gone is the night when all felt hopeless.

Hope rises with the sun.

You call us now to turn again,

Hand in hand to face the dawn.

10.

Bless us as the day begins.

May it be a pleasure, not a fight.

Grant us the grace to start again.

Be with us in our day.

11.

Be in the middle.

Be at the edge.

Be at our borders.

Be in our hearts.

12.

Let us be content just to be.

To be at peace in this place.

Not to strive or to tussle.

To feel held in your love.

13.

God of joy, God of Hope,

God of the lonely,

God of the lost,

Be God to us wherever we are.

14.

Bless us with friends that are virtual.

May we know their love is real.

Hands across the internet

Holding on to what is true.

15.

Make this a home for the homeless.

A destination for the aimless.

A shelter for the weather beaten.

A sanctuary for the lost.

16.

Bless us as we sit here

Staring at a screen.

May the words we read be real to us.

May we feel your presence here.

17.

May this new day bring new hope,

A new enthusiasm for all that life can

bring.

A peace that warms us like the sun.

The strength to carry on.

ALTERNATIVE NIGHT BLESSINGS

1.

As the sun sinks on the day,

Keep our hearts afloat.

Let this night time be our harbour,

A shelter until dawn.

2.

Tell us a story, Jesus,

To see us through the night.

Keep the candle burning.

Like newborns, let us rest.

3.

Your love is like a lullaby:

Soothing, restful, calm.

Enough to see us through the night,

Bring us safely home.

4.

Let sleep run through our bodies.

Flush out the failings of this day,

Bring strength to start over.

Tomorrow IS another day.

5.

When darkness is all around us

It is not the end of the world.

It is no cause for panic,

It is merely the middle of night.

6.

Evening shadows grow longer
And our thoughts turn to sleep.
Grant us a restful night, Lord.
Watch over us till morning.

7.

Let us not toss and turn
But may we sleep in peace.
Waking bright and early
To walk the roads with you.

8.

Tender is the night
That calls us forth to sleep.
To rest and wake refreshed,
Unbowed to face the day.

9.

Lamplighter, lover, friend.

Watch over us tonight.

Keep away our monsters.

Bring us safely home.

10.

Shush now, enough for today.

All will be well by morning.

No more questions for tonight.

We'll start again at dawn.

11.

As night draws near, be with us.

As sleep draws near, grant us rest.

As dreams draw near, may they bring us
comfort.

As rest draws near, grant us peace.

12.

Even if we have failed today

We know you have not given up on us.

Grant us rest this coming night

And a new day to start again.

13.

May his arms enfold you,

His comfort soothe you,

His truth affirm you

And his strength uphold you

Tonight and always.

14.

May his hope be in your heart,

His blessing on your lips,

His peace be all around you

And his joy be in your dawn.

15.

Fill up our emptiness,

Warm our cold hearts,

Chase away our fears,

Bring us safely home.

16.

It is your love that gives us value,

Your truth that gives us hope,

Your words that carry meaning

And your resurrection that brings new life.

17.

Tired limbs, tired hearts,

Weary bones and minds.

Take them all and make them new.

Grant us peace this night.

18.

May He bless you,

Keep you safe,

Calm the waters,

Grant us peace.

FINAL
THOUGHTS

REBECCA'S STORY

Rebecca says:

At the end of 2020, I was in an interesting place. Despite trying to root in multiple churches in my adult life, led to each one by God and growing spiritually within each one, I always seemed to leave under painful circumstances. Issues of discrimination, inclusion, harmful theology cropped up time and time again.

I challenged and unlearned so much from my own conservative upbringing, yet was leading worship within environments expecting me to adhere to cishet norms and purity culture without question. Something had to give. I left organised faith and became a wilderness child.

Ever faithful, God still kept a guiding hand on my life. I saw a worship leader's course advertised, usually based on-site in Scotland but this year running online due to Covid restrictions. Taking the opportunity to do something which would keep me engaged with worship, I signed up. It was a wonderful experience, and I learned so much while also gaining validation that despite messages I had been given, I was gifted as a worship leader in many ways.

Yet I had no intention of going back into on-site church to use that gift. I could not be fully myself within the traditional mechanisms of established church institutions while ableism, homophobia, sexism and racism abounded.

Increasingly, I had become aware of Dave and The Ordinary Office through my growing use of online mediums to explore and engage with other deconstructing Christians. I offered to send in some Christmas Carols I had recorded for his Christmas Service that year, and to support him in editing the copy for the book he wanted to publish.

As we talked more, we two outspoken bolshy Geordies discovered we were kindred spirits and God had absolutely brought us together; Dave needed an ally and I needed an outlet. So, we began to work more closely together, and the next phase of The Ordinary Office was born.

When all seems lost, God continues to hold the threads of the tapestry which is our lives. I didn't know God was setting me up for a ministry I had no idea was even in existence, yet this glistening golden and red thread that is The Ordinary Office was poised in their hands. Thank God for their faithfulness, and thank you, community, for your acceptance.

I truly hope this book has been a blessing to you, and you have found God in these pages as I have in putting them together.

Peace be with you.

GOODBYE

The time has come to go.

To say farewell and walk on.

A casual smile, a gentle kiss,

For my journey carries on.

I walk this pilgrim road

By myself yet not alone.

Others come alongside me

And share the road awhile,

But their journey is not mine.

Though for a time our paths are the same

Eventually our roads will fork.

Yet our paths have somehow become

intertwined,

Our souls connected yet apart.

I will carry you sometimes as you will

carry me,

But we face the cross alone.

I thank you for a journey shared,
For support and friendship on the way.
Until we meet again
In this world or the next.

Peace be with you.

Amen.

APPENDIX 1: HELPERS

https://www.helplines.org/helplines
Directory of helplines accessible across
the UK.

https://hubofhope.co.uk
Directory of support providers, searchable
by type of need.

IAPT (Improving Access to Psychological
Therapies)
Self-referral via www.nhs.uk.

Contact the Samaritans if you need
emergency support, on 116 123 or
jo@samaritans.org

APPENDIX 2: REFERENCES

Berger, Peter L. (1979) *The Heretical Imperative: Contemporary Possibilities of Religious Affirmation.* New York: Anchor Press

Lamsa, George M. (1985) *Holy Bible: From the Ancient Eastern Text: George M. Lamsa's Translation from the Aramaic of the Peshitta.* New York: Harper & Row

Rupp, E. G & Drewery, Benjamin (1970) *Martin Luther, Documents of Modern History.* London: Edward Arnold. p. 42

The Holy Bible: NIV (2021) London: Hodder & Stoughton

The Holy Bible: NIRV (2014) by Biblica, Inc.®. Used by permission. All rights reserved worldwide

NOTES:

NOTES:

NOTES:

NOTES: